THE LIFE OF

Including His Miracles and Parables

Written by Carol Ann Morrow

Illustrated by Ave O. Macasiray

The birthday of Jesus is celebrated on December 25. This is his baby picture. Can you draw him some presents in the boxes?

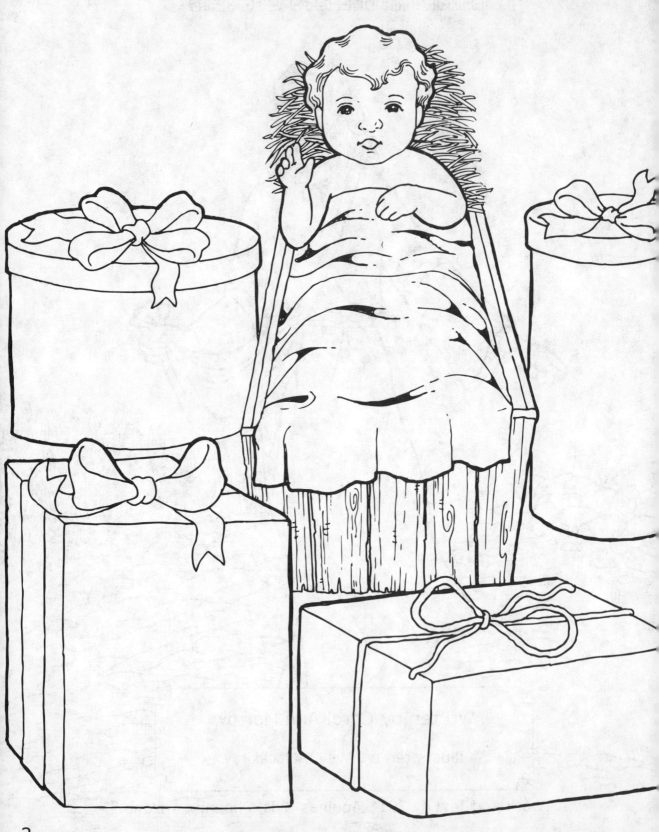

Angels sang to tell the shepherds that Jesus was born. The shepherds came to see this special baby.

Three Wise Men saw a star over the stable where Jesus was born. They came to bring him presents too.

When Jesus was just a baby, Mary and Joseph took him to the Temple to give thanks to God. Simeon and Anna, who were very wise, welcomed Jesus. They knew he would be important to all people.

Mary and Joseph took Jesus with them to Jerusalem every year to celebrate the feast of Passover. They were celebrating the escape of their people from slavery in Egypt.

At the end of their trip to the Temple when Jesus was 12, Mary and Joseph went home while Jesus stayed behind to listen to the teachers and ask them questions. Mary and Joseph looked for Jesus everywhere. Can you find him?

When Mary and Joseph found Jesus, they took him home. They loved and cared for Jesus, who obeyed them and seemed to grow more loving and wise every year.

When Mary looked at her Son, she thought of his unusual birth. She reflected on all that had happened and wondered what would become of her Son when he grew up.

Jesus' cousin John helped prepare the world for Jesus by telling people to get ready. Jesus asked John to baptize him. A voice from heaven said, "You are my beloved Son."

Mary asked Jesus to work his very first miracle at a wedding in Cana. The wine ran out, but Jesus blessed water which turned into wine. Much later, he turned wine into his very own Blood!

A soldier told Jesus that his young servant was paralyzed and that he knew Jesus could cure him without even seeing him. The boy got better. Jesus wants us to trust in Him like that soldier did.

When a widow told Jesus that her young son was about to be buried, Jesus touched his body and the boy stood up and spoke. Jesus loved children. He loves you.

When some Apostles were in a boat during a storm, Jesus walked to them on the water. Peter couldn't believe it, so Jesus invited him to walk on the water too. Jesus said, "Don't be afraid."

Thousands of people followed Jesus to hear him teach. At lunchtime, they were hungry. Jesus blessed a few fish and some loaves of bread and it was enough for everyone! Jesus gives us what we need.

When the Apostles could catch no fish, Jesus said, "Try again."
Then they caught so many fish that the nets could hardly hold
them. Fill the nets in the picture with lots of fish. Put some in
the boat too.

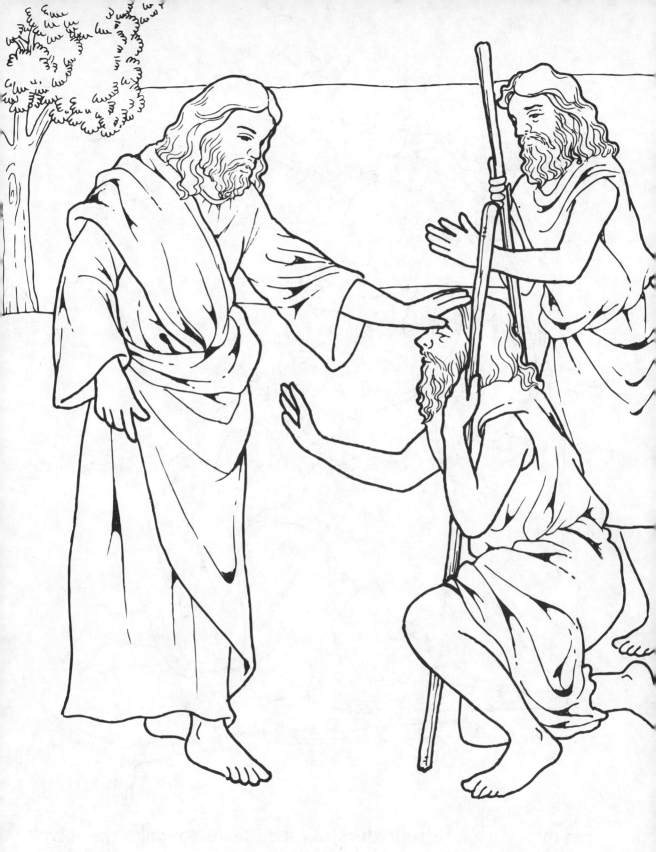

Two blind men waited by the road to ask Jesus to open their eyes. Jesus did. He wants you to look around and see his work everywhere. Draw something wonderful you can see.

Ten men with a terrible disease asked Jesus to make them well. Jesus did. Only one came back to say thank you. Jesus praised this man. He wants us to be thankful for any good things that happen to us.

Jesus' friend Lazarus was buried but his sisters, Mary and Martha, knew that Jesus could bring him back to life. Jesus did this. Jesus gives us life.

Jesus taught with stories called parables. He held up a mustard seed, which is very tiny. That seed, he said, can become such a big bush that birds can nest in it. Circle all the birds in this bush.

Jesus said that if he had lots of sheep but one got lost, he would leave all the rest and hunt for the one that was missing. Can you find a lost sheep in this picture?

Jesus said he was the Good Shepherd. He would fight off the wolf that tried to kill his sheep, even if he was in danger. Jesus wants to protect us from danger. Find the dangers and mark them with an X.

Jesus said that a farmer scattered seeds on the path, on the rocks, in the weeds and in good soil. Draw plants in the place where they will grow best. Jesus wants His words to take root in your heart.

Jesus told of a man beaten by robbers and left bleeding on the road. Some people pretended not to see him, but one man was very kind. Jesus said that the kind man was a good neighbor. Jesus wants you to be kind to others.

Jesus told a story of a young man who ran away and wasted a lot of his Dad's money. He came home sad and said he was sorry. His father hugged him and had a party. When you make a mistake, God still loves you.

Jesus tells us that when we help other people, we are helping Him. This is what He wants us to do.

When Jesus came into Jerusalem for the Feast of Passover, many people shouted Hosanna (Hurray) and waved branches just like you might wave a flag in a parade. Will you march with Jesus now?

On Thursday evening, Jesus celebrated the Passover Supper with his 12 Apostles. He took bread, blessed it, broke it, and said, "Take this and eat it. This is my Body." Then he took a cup of wine and said, "Take this, and drink it. This is my Blood. Do this in memory of me." Jesus invites us to receive Him at Mass in Holy Communion.

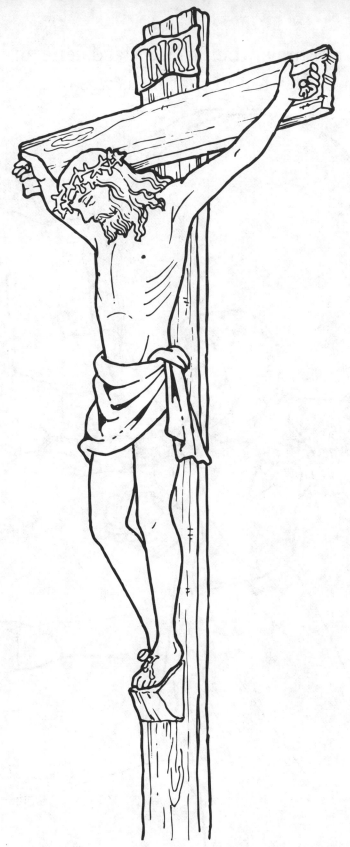

On Friday at noon, Jesus was nailed to a cross where he died three hours later. One of the soldiers cried out, "Clearly this man was the Son of God!" Jesus gave his life because He loved us.

On Sunday morning, when Mary Magdalene and others came to visit the tomb, they found that Jesus was not there. He had risen from the dead!

Forty days after Easter, Jesus gave His Apostles a final blessing and was taken up to heaven. We call this the Ascension.

Today we believe that God continues to be present in our world through His Holy Spirit, through the Gospels, and through the Sacraments of His Church. Jesus is with you now!